First Edition

Published by Palmglen Limited

Palmglen Limited
47 Frith Street
London
W1D 4HT

020 7432 0747

All photographs credited to:

© **John 'Hoppy' Hopkins, 2009**

© **Val Wilmer, 2009**

© **David Redfern, 2009**

© **Allan Titmuss, 2009**

© **David Sinclair, 2009**

Foreword text copyright © **Sally Greene, 2009**

All text copyright © **John Fordham, 2009**

All design and artwork copyright: © **Palmglen Limited**

Printed and bound in Italy by Printer Trento S.r.l
in association with Access Plus.

ISBN  978-0-9563096-0-0

**FRONT COVER DESIGN** : ANDREW GREETHAM

**RONNIE SCOTT** AND **PETE KING** : BACK COVER
Ph. DAVID REDFERN

**GEORGIE FAME'S HAMMOND** : PREVIOUS PAGE
Ph. DAVID SINCLAIR

Mixed Sources
Product group from well-managed forests and other controlled sources
www.fsc.org  Cert no. CQ-COC-000012
© 1996 Forest Stewardship Council
FSC

"I love this place, it's just like home. Filthy, and full of strangers".

RONNIE SCOTT

# RONNIE SCOTT'S AT FIFTY

We would love to have printed a picture or told a story about everyone who has contributed to the life of Ronnie Scott's club, from the most modest sidemen to the biggest international stars. But even to list the names of all the people, from the musical giants to the bar-staff, who've contributed to the  spirit of Ronnie's, would run to far more pages than space allows. As with every personal selection, a different group of people would have chosen differently. But we sincerely hope that all the deserving many that we had to leave out will still find special memories stirred by the images and stories here, and remain rightly proud of their contribution, however big or small, to 'the best jazz club in the world.'

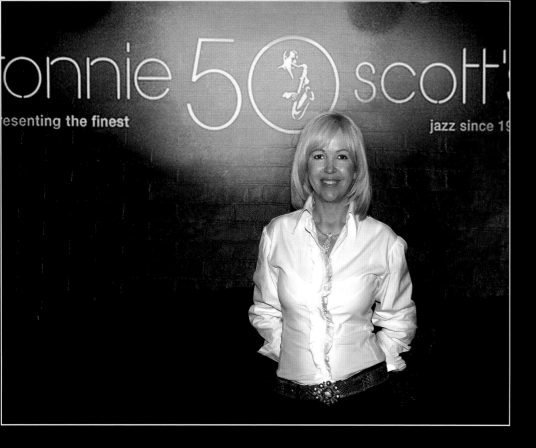

**SALLY GREENE - NEW KEEPER OF THE KEYS AT RONNIE SCOTT'S...**

**SHE OPENED THE DOOR A LITTLE WIDER!**

Ph. DAVID SINCLAIR

Ronnie Scott's is all about jazz, and jazz is all about change. When jazz musicians adopt a favourite song they make it their own, but the song is still the song albeit presented in a different way. I hope that I've kept the songs and music of the founders of this incredible jazz club, Ronnie and Pete. And although there have been a few modulations along the way, there have been no major transformations.

I love music - jazz, blues, funk, bebop and soul - and I know great music when I hear it, but I leave the labels to the historians. Where there are labels there are barriers. Ronnie's is about great jazz played by great musicians to a global and multicultural audience and especially with so much British talent around, the thrill is just to get out there and see someone you've never even heard of and be completely blown away.

In 2005, I heard that Ronnie's needed a new keeper of the keys (because that's all I am) and I was thrilled to take on the monumental task of following in the footsteps of the greatest jazz venue in the world, where Nina Simone sang the blues raw and oh so soulful, where the incredible Miles Davis took some beating. My piano teacher says I sound like Thelonious Monk, but I don't think he means it as a compliment... Monk's playing can be jarring and dissonant! It's incredible to watch James Pearson, one of the most brilliant jazz pianists, Guy Barker, an amazing British trumpet player, and our fantastic young jazz musicians Michael Mwenso and Jay Phelps, teaching kids who desperately want to learn an instrument that they can't afford to pick up. Tap Jam, indie films about jazz, late night jam sessions at Ronnie's bar... there is always a new way to celebrate.

I have run theatres and worked with actors in plays and musicals, and it's clear that the theatre and the jazz world have always had plenty in common. Actors and jazz musicians especially. Both are still treated as outsiders. Both have to know how to improvise. Both have to reach out and grab the audience. Both rely heavily on discipline, technique, rhythm, timing, interpretation and ensemble playing - these are essential ingredients in any piece of theatre - and a large part of jazz repertoire originated in the theatre. Our audiences come with an open mind to see or hear something nobody has seen or heard of before. It's an energy that steals away your blues for just a moment. I bow to the integrity and tenacity of Ronnie and Pete and I hope that they are still proud of the greatest jazz club in the world...

I've taken away the chewing gum, put ice in the drinks, and seemed to have perfected the best chip in Soho (so that I can disprove Ronnie's theory about the flies). I want to thank all those who have contributed and the people who have followed my dream over the last four years. To all the professionals who have looked and booked, the artists who have brought their energy and passion to Ronnie's stage, to the media who have supported us over the years, to our customers, the staff, and all those who have helped keep this Club's soul intact - thank you for realising this dream.

**Sally Greene**
September 2009

Joe Zawinul, one of the jazz music's greatest surviving legends, put his finger on the magic of Ronnie Scott's Club in this 50th anniversary year. 'This place is almost unique now,' Zawinul told a packed house one night in a sensational run of performances by the pianist's Syndicate band in May 2004. 'There aren't many jazz clubs like it left in the world.'

The late Ronnie Scott, the club's co-founder and proprietor, used to think highly of it too, in his way. 'I love this place, it's just like home,' he used to tell his listeners. 'Filthy, and full of strangers. Last night vandals broke in and redecorated it.'

But if he kept his deepest emotions about his club well disguised, Ronnie Scott undoubtedly did love it, and a home to him it certainly was. The photographs of all the jazz stars on the walls - Ella Fitzgerald, Sonny Rollins, Coleman Hawkins, Ben Webster, Bill Evans, and dozens of others - could have been pictures of family members, and in a way they were. Joe Zawinul picked up on their importance at once. Looking around at the photographs, Zawinul said: 'A lot of clubs might put pictures up like those, for the atmosphere. But there's a big difference in this club. Most of those people have actually played here.'

Ronnie Scott's is the most famous jazz club on the planet, respected by fans and performers alike. Impoverished students sharing a drink, office parties on the razzle, dedicated fans straining to catch every sound, the occasional movie star or Cabinet Minister, they all rub shoulders without fear or favour in Ronnie's, and no-one is above the iron law of the establishment - that the music comes first and you're expected to respect it. The signboard by the entrance testifies to that, still namechecking everyone performing that night, whether in the headline band or the supporting group.

The name of Ronnie Scott's is now known all over the world, even to those who might hardly ever visit a jazz club or buy a jazz album. Ask a London cab-driver to take you to Ronnie Scott's, and they won't need the name of the street. They're also quite likely to ask you 'who's on tonight?'. And even if they haven't heard of the artist, they'll know that if it's on at Ronnie's, it's got to be good. Ronnie Scott's Club is dedicated to jazz as the most exciting and influential music of the past hundred years, and the creation of near-perfect conditions in which to play it and hear it, that has brought the club its global reputation.

**JOE ZAWINUL** with
**PETE KING** 2002
Ph. DAVID SINCLAIR

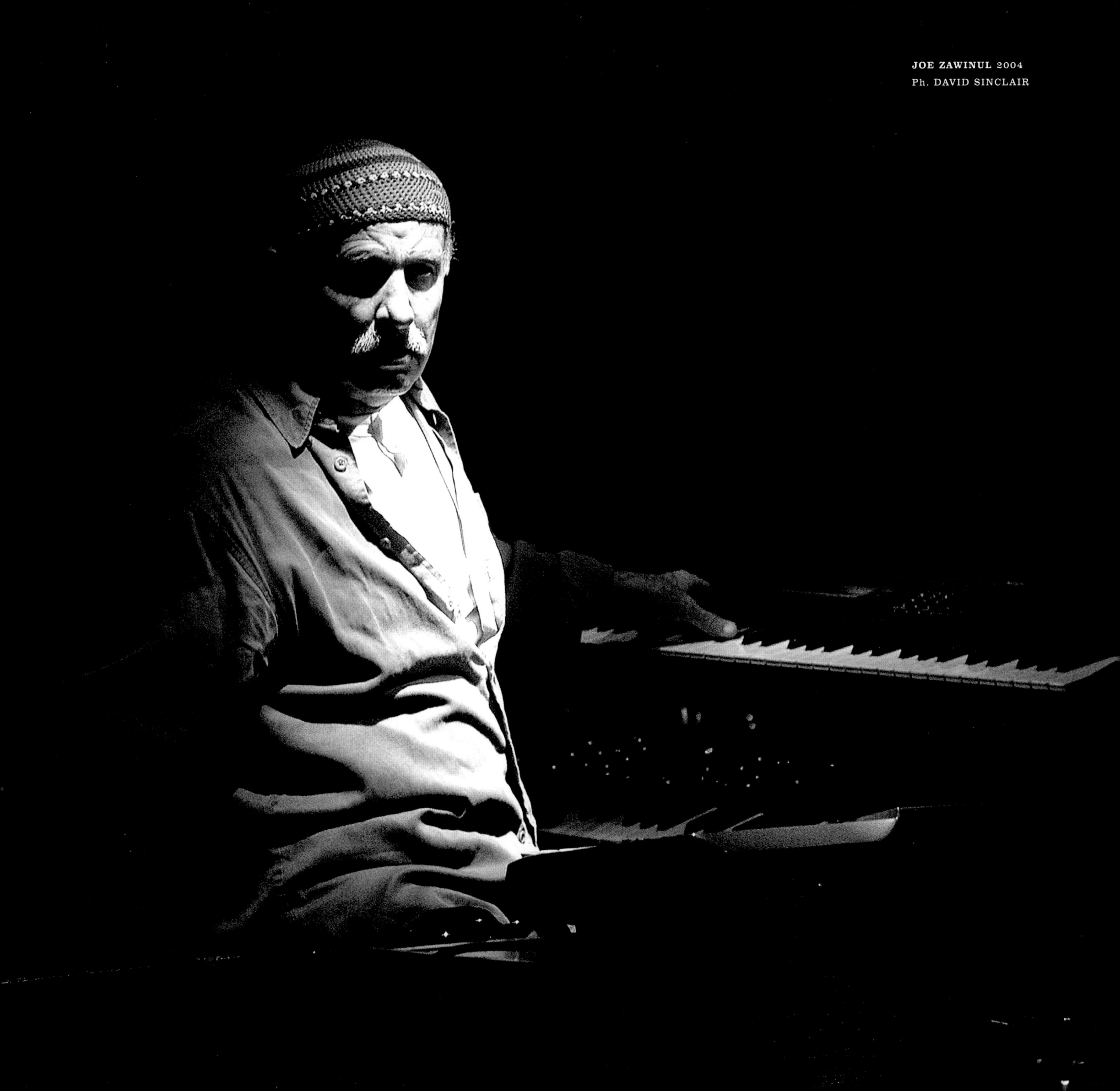

**JOE ZAWINUL** 2004
Ph. DAVID SINCLAIR

What was desperately needed in London
in the 1950s was a specialist jazz club,

Fifty years ago, things were a little different. The premises were not in Frith Street then, but in a tatty basement a few blocks away in Gerrard Street, in the heart of London's Chinatown. The bar served tea, not alcohol, and there were no waiters or waitresses. The artists' dressing-room doubled as the club's office, at the front of the club beneath the street - musicians had to wind their way through the fans to get to the stage. But in the quality of the jazz played there, and in the character of the proprietor Ronnie Scott - who combined the skills of a world-class saxophone player with a dry stand-up wit worthy of Jack Dee - the club had a unique character even from its modest early days, before that glittering procession of international stars had begun to arrive.

The establishing of a specialist club devoted to modern jazz in London was a triumph of blind optimism over economic realities. This was the late 1950s, when the whirlwind that was rock'n'roll had already been overtaking the commercial popularity of jazz for some years, and didn't look like going away. Upmarket nightclubs, restaurants and the dance-hall circuit certainly still presented jazz, but it needed to be the kind the passing punter could easily relate to - and dance to - rather than the purer version favoured by the hardline fan with a photographic memory for the catalogue numbers of obsolete discs.

A twenty-something Ronnie Scott and his circle of elite British modernists weren't in the jazz-anorak category, but they were certainly fans as much as players. Their world was very different, though, from that of the trad-jazz scene of the time, on which bearded, baggy-jumpered men took time out from jobs as librarians and engineers to try to recreate what they imagined had been the authentic sound of old New Orleans. But modern jazz was strictly a professional activity. The players were taking time out too, of course, from jobs as West End orchestra-pit or dance-band sidemen, cruise-ship entertainers, studio session specialists. And they were frustrated by the lack of opportunities to play the 'real jazz' they knew was happening on the other side of the Atlantic - a fierce new jazz, played at the edge of the envelope. Some of them tried to smuggle the new bebop of Charlie Parker and Dizzy Gillespie into their commercial work and hope the boss didn't notice, but that was a risky adventure that could get you fired.

What was desperately needed in London in the 1950s was a specialist jazz club, a place run by fans for fans - or by musicians for musicians, which is how Ronnie Scott's Club came into existence in the first place.

When the 1950s dawned, Ronnie Scott was a charismatic 23 year-old tenor saxophonist from the East End, who had already been making waves on the British jazz scene since his late teens. His saxophonist father Jock Scott (descended from East European Jewish émigrés, and originally named Joseph Schatt) had left home when Ronnie was a child, but as a well-known dance-band musician was a powerful background presence. Scott's mother Cissie and grandmother Becky doted on the boy, and had bought him a brand-new sax and lessons from an expert as soon as he had shown an interest in music. When he was eighteen, a fast-learning Ronnie Scott had been hired by the internationally famous Ted Heath dance orchestra (though he was subsequently fired for playing bebop in it), and as a good-looking, sharp-dressing, wise-cracking performer with the skills to match the all-conquering Americans, he was the new kid on the block everybody had noticed.

At the time, the only home for London bebop players seeking relief from the tedious routines of dance-band music was a shabby basement called Mac's Rehearsal Rooms, opposite the Windmill Theatre. It was just a cramped, low-ceilinged room with a bandstand at one end, dimly lit by bare bulbs, and with a few battered sofas passing for the soft furnishings. But it was the perfect location, being around the corner from Archer Street, the jazz and dance-band musicians' outdoor social club and informal job-centre, where they would swap news of opportunities and gigs, and pit-band fixers would sign up players for West End shows.

Ronnie Scott led a band at Mac's, and so did a classically-trained clarinet and sax prodigy from Essex, altoist John Dankworth. Mac's Rehearsal Rooms became an out-of-hours jamming haunt, then a regular jazz club called Club Eleven, in honour of its ten regular players plus the non-playing photographer and jazz fan Harry Morris, who ran the box-office. Run-down and unprepossessing as it was, the Club Eleven became the first live-music establishment in Britain to present an all-jazz repertoire with a policy devised entirely by a co-operative of professional players.

Word about the Club Eleven got around. Even American musicians passing through London, including bandleaders Benny Goodman and Tadd Dameron, and singer Ella Fitzgerald, had heard about the place and dropped by. The founders dreamed of a place that might resemble the thrilling back-to-back jazz clubs of New York's 52nd Street, which they had begun to discover on trips to New York as dance-band entertainers on the Transatlantic liners.

The Club Eleven closed down in 1950, following a widely-publicised police raid for drugs ('Police Swoop on a Soho Bebop Club!' shouted the Evening News). Ronnie Scott became a full-time bandleader, going on the road with a very successful nine-piece combination of Mecca Ballrooms dance-band music and as much real jazz as he could get away with. In the nine-piece was a kindred spirit with whom Ronnie Scott shared an attitude to music, and a sense of humour - a young fellow-tenorist called Pete King. It was to become a lifelong friendship, and a business partnership that led to the founding of what many believe to be the best jazz club in the world.

Despite a veneer of lazy charm that could make him seem indifferent to most things that didn't involve race-courses, saxophones or the opposite sex, Ronnie Scott was in his way a driven man. He had fallen in love with the atmosphere of the New York jazz clubs from his first visit at the end of the 1940s. In 1959, he and King heard of the availability of a shabby, dimly-lit basement in Gerrard Street, owned by a small-time Soho businessman by the name of Jack Fordham.

During World War Two, 39 Gerrard Street had been a bottle-party club, and later a refuge for cab drivers for card-games and coffee, and a 'near-beer' joint, in which male customers would be encouraged by the apparent friendliness of the waitresses to spend a fortune in the mistaken assumption that the waitresses might become even friendlier at the end of the night. But Jack Fordham was losing interest in the place, and in 1959 decided to cut his losses, offering it to Scott and King for a knockdown rent. Scott borrowed £1000 from his stepfather Sol Berger, who ran a textiles business and had supported the saxophonist's career from the beginning.

On October 31 1959, the following advertisement appeared in Melody Maker:

# RONNIE SCOTT'S CLUB
## 39 Gerrard Street, W1

**OPENING TONIGHT!**
Friday 7:30pm.

Tubby Hayes Quartet: the trio with
Eddie Thompson, Stan Roberts, Spike Heatley.

A young alto saxophonist, Peter King, and
an old tenor saxophonist, Ronnie Scott.

The first appearance in a jazz club since the
relief of Mafeking by Jack Parnell.

Membership 10/- until January 1961.
Admission 1/6 (to members) 2/6 (non-members)

The entry concluded boldly: 'The best jazz in the best club in town'. It was a piece of hype, included on the grounds that you didn't lose anything by exaggeration. But it turned out to be nothing less than the truth.

Ronnie Scott's Jazz Club
39 Gerrard Street
London W1

That first night was a sensation, mingling the flying virtuosity of young sax prodigy Tubby Hayes, the polished modern-swing of pianist Eddie Thompson, and Ronnie Scott's customary lyrical elegance. And there was a teenage newcomer who was to make a formidable international impact in the years to come - a shy 19 year-old alto sax sensation from Surrey, also called Peter King, whose grasp of the complexities of Charlie Parker's playing made the jaws of even hardened pros drop.

Melody Maker splashed pictures of the opening weekend's performers in its next edition, and called Peter King 'the new alto sensation.' As for Ronnie Scott's friend and business partner of the same name, it lessened at least some of the confusion over their identities that the older man had now stopped playing professionally and was devoting himself entirely to management. From the beginning, it was an unspoken agreement between Scott and King that the former would be the club's frontman, presenter and public face, and the latter would manage 'the office'. Scott's creativity, wit and intuitions but indifference to fine detail and small print, and King's self-taught business acumen, made it the perfect partnership to run as eccentric a business as a jazz club.

But the first night was the easy part. Now they had to keep it up, week in, week out. They ran shows every evening and spent the days trying to improve the premises. Pete King's carpenter father-in-law made some rudimentary furniture. They found a wholesaler who would provide the staple drink - tea - by the vanload. They learned fast, and quickly discovered some fundamental problems about jazz promoting. One was the unevenness of the audiences across the week. Fridays and Saturdays would do good business, but the average week-night could be a graveyard. There was also a law of diminishing returns about presenting the same local jazz artists, however good, to the same fans night after night. A third problem was the lack of a licensed bar.

Scott and King took a friend, the saxophonist and journalist Benny Green (as a literary man, they thought he might present a more reassuring image) when they made an official application to the police for a liquor license. 'What is the purpose of this club?' a weary officer asked the applicants. 'To try to get rhythm sections to play in time,' Green had replied, stone-faced - a statement that was meticulously noted down. The installation of a fire-escape turned out to be the only condition for approval of the license. The jazzmen solved this by extending a ladder upstairs into the hallway of the garment manufacturer on the next floor up - a precarious escape route made worse by the periodic standoffs between the jazz musicians and their neighbours above. The clothes-manufacturer was furious about noise from rehearsals at the club in the afternoons. The argument even went to court, with the plaintiffs complaining about the racket from 'buglers' downstairs. Scott, Benny Green and a council official with a noise-meter spent much time skulking in the upstairs passage gathering evidence. On that occasion, jazz-singing superstar Ella Fitzgerald was in town, and using the club for rehearsals in the afternoon. Some opined that the neighbours should have felt privileged rather than inconvenienced by the sound from such a star, but in any event Benny Green later wrote that the noise-meter barely registered even the sound of 'our own heavy breathing.'

Ronnie Scott's Club began to gain a kind of bohemian respectability. Colin McInnes, writer of the novels 'Absolute Beginners' and 'City of Spades' was a friend of former Club Eleven pianist Denis Rose. MacInnes was a jazz-fan, and a regular attender. So was actor and playwright Harold Pinter. But, then as later, Scott and King didn't care whether their regulars were famous or obscure, as long as they added a little colour and unpredictability to life, and listened to the music. A man called Fred Twigg attached himself to the club, and became its odd-job man and cleaner. He took to sleeping on the premises, and because he was plagued by imaginary apparitions, often complained to the proprietors about flying creatures and demented gorillas he claimed frequented the establishment at night.

Afternoon rehearsals as a source of income extended to an actors' group that included at various times Maggie Smith, George Devine of the Royal Court Theatre, Michael Caine and Lindsay Anderson. Scott and Benny Green found the rehearsals irresistible. They were happy to endlessly make tea for the performers and watch in awe. The high dramatic style was catching. Scott would ask Green such questions as 'what dost thou fancy in the 4.30?' George Devine once set up an exercise in body-language in which he demanded that the actors wore masks and then guess each other's emotions without the help of facial expression. A masked and threatening-looking Devine went up the stairs into Gerrard Street and was promptly assaulted by various paranoid Soho passers-by. When he broke free and ran petrified back down into the basement, the waiting actors, carrying out his instructions to the letter, all shouted 'fear'.

Ronnie Scott had a knack for public relations, a skill that had proved useful since the beginnings of his bandleading days in the 1950s. His advertisements in Melody Maker became a miniature art-form. He would claim that the club would be featuring an unexpected joint appearance by Sir Thomas Beecham, Somerset Maugham and Little Richard. He would promise food untouched by human hands because the chef was a gorilla.

Neither of the proprietors had much of a business strategy, beyond adding up the takings at the end of each week and figuring out if it was enough to stay open for the next. Throughout 1960, this policy just about worked. But a constant menu of local jazz musicians was approaching its sell-by date. As they had done all their jazz-playing lives, Scott and King turned their gaze once again toward America.

The pre-war Musicians' Union ban, set up to protect British musicians' jobs by keeping American players out, was already easing by this time. International jazz artists were regularly visiting Britain by 1960 for one-off concerts or tours. But the notion of a nightclub residency lasting a week or several weeks, was still off the agenda. Pete King began to put out feelers, and found the British union tentatively agreeable, if an exchange deal involving a British member could be worked out. King thought the most likely candidate was London's hottest saxophonist, Tubby Hayes. He offered Hayes to the Cantorino brothers, who ran New York's Half Note club - in exchange for one of their most popular attractions, the former Woody Herman and Stan Kenton saxophonist Zoot Sims, a man who reflected much of the straightahead, good-humoured swing and bebop sophistication that Ronnie Scott practised himself. The Cantorinos bought the idea, and eventually so did the redoubtable James 'Little Caesar' Petrillo and the American Federation of Musicians. King rang Ronnie Scott in London to tell him the good news. The swap was arranged for November 1961.

Ronnie Scott's Club was about to become an international jazz venue.

Zoot Sims did everything the proprietors could have asked of him. He swung hard, his ideas seemed inexhaustible, he made a simple repertoire of standard songs and blues sound new, he was funny and good company, and he liked the club. Sims occupied Gerrard Street throughout the month of November 1961 playing to thrilled audiences - the only doubter was the hallucinating cleaner Fred Twigg, who for some reason was convinced Sims was a Russian secret agent.

The musicians' unions' numbers game was strictly interpreted back then. If one player was going from Britain to the States, only one could come the other way. Sims couldn't bring a band he was used to (Scott and King couldn't have afforded it anyway), he had to come as a 'single' and play with a local house band. This was a potential minefield for a jazz-club proprietor, particularly given the gap between the standards of American rhythm-sections and most European ones at that time.

But Scott and King were fortunate to chance on a secret weapon. Stan Tracey. Most British jazz musicians and fans were in awe of Americans then, but if Tracey was awed by anything, he never showed it. A one-time teenage accordion player in the forces entertainment network ENSA - where he worked with the comedians Tony Hancock and Bob Monkhouse - Tracey had been steadily developing as a Thelonious Monk and Duke Ellington-influenced pianist of rugged character through the 1950s, and he was already regularly recording under his own name. Tracey and Zoot Sims quickly hit it off, and the pianist's mix of sympathetic listening and challenging inventiveness stimulated the American without getting in his way. It was a trick Tracey was to pull off with many star visitors over the coming years. Sims and Tracey even made an album while the saxophonist was in England. This was a landmark in itself, because recordings of British modernists with their American counterparts were virtually unheard of.

News of the charms of 39 Gerrard Street was getting around. Zoot Sims had told the British press that the place had much of the downbeat atmosphere of a New York jazz club. Some found its tattiness and lack of pretensions also echoed the run-down but exciting London bottle-party joints of the war years. It was a below-stairs night-time dive, it had a whiff of nonconformity and danger about it. A loudspeaker at the top of the rickety stairway, relaying music from the depths, beckoned potential punters - or sometimes provided the whole show for those who were too poor or too young to get in. Fans loved the proximity to the guests, the way they would be ushered from the cubby-hole under the street they flatteringly called 'the office' through the parting crowd, up to the tiny stage to pick up one of Stan Tracey's quirky, sidelong piano introductions. Local musicians liked the club as a place to meet friends, maybe stay on for an after-hours jam session. Ronnie Scott's offstage antics as a mimic, a clown and an unfazeably quick wit (he was always far more spontaneously and creatively funny than his practised standup routine at the club made him seem) was another attraction for the insiders.

But having got a taste of the international potential, audiences now expected something as good as Zoot Sims, or maybe even better. Lucky Thompson, a saxophonist who had played with Charlie Parker, Miles Davis and Count Basie, soon followed, and was the first African-American to play at Gerrard Street. In September 1962, came the mighty Dexter Gordon - a jazz giant in all senses at six foot five, with a huge, domineering saxophone sound. Scott and Gordon would perform a public charade together in which the proprietor would pretend he didn't have the money for the wages - and it wasn't always a pretence. Gordon's performances were dramatic reminders of why modern jazz worked better as an intimate-venue rather than a concert hall music. The saxophonist was right on top of the entranced audiences, the front row was inches away from his massive flapping feet, the sweat that poured off him and bounced in miniature fountains on the floor.

Even more excitement was generated by the blind multi-instrumentalist Rahsaan Roland Kirk, a former member of the Charles Mingus band. Kirk could play three-part harmonies on three saxes at once, and could also scat-sing along with his own improvised solos on a flute. Kirk was a very rare breed - an allround entertainer who could play first-class jazz, and remain true to his principles and the music's history. But he was suspicious with Scott and King at first, demanding his money in cash every night. These were doubts born out of plenty of bitter experiences with club-owners, and Scott and King understood them. But within days of realising he was working for fellow-enthusiasts and players, who understood what a working musician's life was like, Kirk relaxed. It was to be the first of many occasions on which a potentially awkward situation was defused by the club's special character as an establishment run by musicians, that put musicians' needs as high in its priorities as those of the paying customers.

Kirk went on being one of the club's biggest draws for years. The showmanship of his street-busker image and spectacular multi-instrumentalism brought crowds, though his take on jazz was much deeper. And when Kirk was around, things happened. He used to pass whistles out to the crowd to help him on a favourite tune, 'Here Comes the Whistle Man'. In the early 1960s, the instruments sounded much the same as the police whistles the force used to summon aid. The police decided to raid the place in search of liquor-license infringements - entering ostentatiously and blowing whistles - one night during Kirk's performance of his own whistle piece. The blind saxophonist thought the whistle chorus was simply audience enthusiasm, and resolutely went on playing. 'Tell that man to stop playing,' an agitated police officer demanded of Pete King over the noise. 'You tell him,' King replied, knowing that Kirk in full cry was pretty much impossible to stop.

News of Kirk reached the Beatles, who came to Gerrard Street to hear him in 1963 - the year in which they had five chart hits. But the Liverpool group's significance to Ronnie Scott's turned out to be much bigger than raising its profile in the press. As British rock'n'roll boomed, the union quota system applying to transatlantic exchanges of players became irrelevant. For the first time, Americans wanted British musicians as fast as they could be packed on to the planes.

In 1964, Scott and King decided to improve the facilities a little. They sent the customers' food orders to the local restaurants for delivery. They repainted the club, with the unexpected help of a famous Soho character called Gypsy Larry - a grey-haired, weatherbeaten old man in a bandana who hung out with a fellow local eccentric called Iron Foot Jack Neave. Iron Foot Jack used to advertise sales of 'The World's Most Daring Book on Sex and Marriage', and then send applicants a copy of the Bible. Gypsy Larry entered the Gerrard Street premises one day, requested a paintbrush to help with the redecorations, and stayed until his death twelve years later. It all became part of the folklore of Ronnie's. Albert Dimes, a famous Soho gangster Ronnie Scott's father Jock had visited the race-tracks with, gave Scott and King a magnum of champagne to open once they started making real money. It gathers dust on a shelf at the back of the current Frith Street premises to this day.

Scott and King were saxophonists and liked saxophonists, so they decided to go on hiring saxophonists until somebody told them different. They got Stan Getz in March 1964, just as the subtle, soft-toned and romantic American musician was on a roll with the commercial popularity of the 'Jazz Samba' album with Brazilians Antonio Carlos Jobim and Astrud Gilberto. 'House Full' notices were up outside 39 Gerrard Street for a month. Getz was at the peak of his form, mesmerising the audience with his lovely tone, and the graceful ease with which he would burnish a song and make it his own. But he could be a hard man to get along with. Getz and Pete King didn't hit it off, and neither did the saxophonist take to Stan Tracey's pungent, idiosyncratic manner of accompaniment. Ronnie Scott slipped a disc getting into his car during this period, and claimed he got it 'bending over backwards to please Stan Getz'.

After Getz came the technically fearsome bebop alto saxist Sonny Stitt, with whom Ronnie Scott got into a long, impromptu saxophone jam one night in 1964, with members of the touring Ray Charles and Dave Brubeck bands dropping by to join in. Scott memorably held his own, despite the competitive Stitt constantly changing the key in mid-flight. Then came Ben Webster, the great tenor sax romantic and former Duke Ellington sideman, blowing delicate smoke-rings of sound that fellow-saxophonists listening considered to be close to miracles.

Theodore Walter 'Sonny' Rollins arrived at the beginning of 1965 - and a regular association with Ronnie Scott's Club began that lasted over a decade and is still spoken of with awe by those who heard him there in those years. Fans would revisit the club three or four times during a Rollins run to hear how differently the same songs would be treated from one night to the next - and his behaviour on the premises could be as startling as his music. Rollins might arrive in a cab, step out of it already playing the tenor, descend the staircase and make his way to the stage still playing. He might leave the bandstand and lead the crowd, Pied Piper-like, out into Gerrard Street, with Stan Tracey's band still pumping away in the basement. Rollins loved weird hats and weirder haircuts - sometimes a Mohican, sometimes a beret, sometimes a Stetson, sometimes a bush hat with corks hanging from it.

Another landmark was passed in March 1965 - the club hired a man who didn't play the saxophone. The studious-looking New Jersey pianist Bill Evans, who had contributed so memorably to Miles Davis's world-famous 'Kind of Blue' album, arrived for a residency - and with his own band, a mark of the club's increasing prosperity and the relaxed Union rules. Evans was such a subtle and delicate player, however, that the proprietors could not contemplate asking him to play on it - Stan Tracey could only play it by having memorised where its faulty notes were.

In the course of trying to hire a grand piano for Evans, Scott and King were reminded of how many people outside the jazz world still seemed to think of the music as something dangerous and strange, its players undisciplined, its audiences unruly. 'Drinks will get spilled on the piano, girls will sit on it', the club proprietors were told by the anxious sales-staff, at one exclusive West End piano showroom. A studio-musician friend eventually came through with the loan of a good instrument, just in time for Evans' season.

Evans' run at the club was a remarkable example of how a great performing artist, however untheatrical or even private in method, could mesmerise an audience. The pianist was thin, intense and bespectacled, and he curled over the keyboard with his nose virtually touching it. His solos were not successions of choruses loosely strung together but intricate and subtle stories, and the Gerrard Street fans were captivated by them. Evans was then followed into the club by one of the greatest guitarists in all jazz. Wes Montgomery was as amiable and outward-going as Evans was turned inward, spinning breezy streams of melody from his guitar as if the activity were as easy and natural as walking.

**VICTOR FELDMAN** 1960
Ph. VAL WILMER

'They called Harold McNair Little Jesus. You could see that in his face. He's in the famous office under the stairs at Gerrard Street, it's a rare picture of it - you can even read the phone number. He was a fine saxophonist and flute-player who had played with the Jamaica All Stars in the 1940s and then become an influential figure over here.'

VAL WILMER

**HAROLD McNAIR** 1960
Ph. VAL WILMER

**RONNIE SCOTT** 1961
Ph. VAL WILMER

**CAB QUAYE** 1961
Ph. VAL WILMER

**ZOOT SIMS** 1961
Ph. VAL WILMER

**LUCKY THOMPSON** 1962
Ph. JOHN 'HOPPY' HOPKINS

**LUCKY THOMPSON** with **STAN TRACEY** on piano 1962
Ph. JOHN 'HOPPY' HOPKINS

**STAN GETZ** 1960s
Ph. VAL WILMER

**DEXTER GORDON** 1962

Ph. VAL WILMER

**JOHNNY GRIFFIN** 1962

Ph. VAL WILMER

**ROLAND KIRK** with
**RONNIE SCOTT** 1963
Ph. JOHN 'HOPPY' HOPKINS

**GERRY MULLIGAN** with
**DAVE BAILEY** on drums 1963
Ph. VAL WILMER

'Bebop musicians tended to dismiss singers, but Babs was a hero, wonderful at that vocalese style of mimicking instruments. He was amazing at finding work too - if he'd found himself on Mars, he could have hustled a gig. He didn't care for the pianist he'd been given at Ronnie's, so he went out into Soho to look for another one - came back saying 'I found this young boy round the corner.' It turned out to be Brian Auger, who became a star.'

VAL WILMER

**BABS GONZALES** with
**MALCOLM CECIL** on bass 1963
Ph. VAL WILMER

**RONNIE SCOTT** and **SONNY STITT** 1964
Ph. VAL WILMER

'Ray Charles was touring Britain, so two of his trumpeters, Roy Burrowes and Oliver Beener, had turned up to sit in with the guitarist Ernest Ranglin at Ronnie's, and so had Dave Brubeck's bassist Gene Wright. Sonny Stitt and Ronnie joined in. The jazz scene was like that then, a lot more impromptu jamming went on.'

VAL WILMER

**OLIVER BEENER,**
**ROY BURROWES** and
**SONNY STITT** 1964
Ph. VAL WILMER

**ERNEST RANGLIN** and
**ROY BURROWES** 1964
Ph. VAL WILMER

**ART FARMER** 1964
Ph. VAL WILMER

**WES MONTGOMERY** 1965
Ph. VAL WILMER

**SONNY ROLLINS** 1965
Ph. VAL WILMER

SONNY ROLLINS 1965
Ph. DAVID REDFERN

**ART BLAKEY** 1965
Ph. VAL WILMER

CHRIS McGREGOR'S BLUE NOTES
DUDU PUKWANA
MONGEZI FEZA
JOHNNY DYANI
CHRIS McGREGOR 1965
Ph. VAL WILMER

Ronnie Scott's Jazz Club
47 Frith Street
London W1

The biggest legends in jazz were now gracing Ronnie Scott's Club constantly. But accompanying the charisma of their music came - air fares, hotels, big fees. However big the name, 39 Gerrard Street couldn't accomodate more than 150 paying admirers. The jazz family was growing. It was time for a bigger home.

In the summer of 1965, the right premises became available a few blocks away at 47 Frith Street, the home of the club today. The space needed investment Scott and King didn't have, but their old friend and admirer, the impresario Harold Davison, came in with a £35,000 loan. And close to six years after Ronnie Scott's Club first opened, the proof that they had made it came on November 27 1965. There were eighteen months still to run on the lease at Gerrard Street, so Scott and King turned the place over to the younger generation of British musicians to perform and rehearse in, providing a performance space for Mike Westbrook, John Surman, John McLaughlin, Mike Gibbs, Graham Collier, Chris McGregor's South African Blue Notes and many others. The 'Old Place' as it came to be called, was the hothouse for a generation of local musicians who no longer looked only to America for inspiration. Its significance in nurturing a truly independent British jazz scene was immense.

Frith Street might have represented a move upmarket, but it didn't make much difference to business as usual behind the scenes. 'The office' at Frith Street was now a back room behind the stage, but it was still cramped, untidy, and full of people who looked as if they'd drifted idly in off the street. Sonny Rollins might be looking in a mirror, performing facial contortions and muttering to himself in a French accent. Pallid individuals looking like minicab drivers awaiting calls might be sitting on upturned instrument cases reading the racing pages or telling deadpan jokes. Pete King might be on the phone, Ronnie Scott watching TV with his feet up on the desk.

It was an atmosphere of informality that was part of the character of the place, though it could be intimidating to outsiders. The ethos of Ronnie Scott's was always that pomposity and rank-pulling were banned, and jazz musicians, of whatever generation, were family. Ronnie Scott's bandleader father Jock's old playing partners from the boats and hotel bands would get a drink on the house, sometimes even a loan if times were hard. Jeff Ellison, a drummer and old Club Eleven associate, became doorman and Ronnie Scott's regular chess partner. The staff could be brusque, even to the customers, but it was a mannerism, not a sign of indifference. Eventually these sometimes offputting practises became known as the curriculum of 'the Frith Street Charm School.'

These were some of the club's best years, and Ronnie Scott's best years too. He was working regularly with his own groups, in the multinational all-star line-up of bebop drum legend Kenny Clarke and Belgian composer Francy Boland, and he would even accept occasional session-work, most famously the sax part on the Beatles 'Lady Madonna'. He would sometimes practice the saxophone walking around the club's empty tables in the afternoons, often perform incomprehensible wind-ups on innocent customers ringing up to book a table, frequently disappear to the betting shop. 'I can stop a runaway horse just by putting money on it,' was Scott's usual assessment of his gambling skills.

He was more than ever the front man, making the announcements and telling jokes, withering in his dismissal of hecklers or drunks in the audience with comebacks like: 'if you want real humour I'll have to dress up in that suit you're wearing', or 'that's OK sir, I remember my first drink.' And the club came to seem more like home than ever, not just to its proprietors, but to many of the touring jazz stars who felt it offered them a place where they were understood, appreciated, accepted for what they were. Coleman Hawkins, a towering giant of the tenor saxophone a couple of decades before, was in his mid-sixties by this time - and appearing to survive only on a diet of Remy Martin brandy and cigarettes, despite the waitresses' attempts to feed him. Ben Webster, another tenor-sax genius, was also a man whose performances could be variable in later years, but Ronnie Scott was unconcerned about inconsistencies from players who seemed like gods to him. In response to complaints that on occasion Webster seemed to ramble more than he blew the saxophone, Scott simply said, 'I'd rather hear Ben Webster talk than ninety per cent of saxophone players play.'

But rock had now irretrievably changed the music business and jazz with it. Miles Davis was experimenting with electronic instruments and rock rhythms in his bands. The reign of the Archer Street dance-band professionals was over. And for all the genius of the performers who continued to come to the club, the audience was becoming harder to please. The jazz-purist ethos of the early days had to change, and the club's approach to become more businesslike. Scott and King formed a booking agency called Ronnie Scott Directions to put the club's guests out on UK tours, and bought the next-door lease (once again with Harold Davison's help) to enlarge the room, a move that also offered an upstairs space to use as a disco. The witty and cantankerous drummer/bandleader Buddy Rich came in to play before the club was really ready to reopen, while cables were still hanging from the ceiling. 'First time I've ever worked in a building site' he told the audience. The BBC filmed a series of concerts at the club for the tenth anniversary celebrations in 1969, including the only performance on the premises by Miles Davis. Ronnie Scott's cornered almost everyone who was ever anyone in jazz, but Davis was always the one who got away.

With its informal atmosphere, and embodiment of the notion that jazz ought to be 'the sound of surprise', Ronnie Scott's continued to be a place where something unexpected could always happen. Jimi Hendrix played there the night before his sudden death in 1970, jamming with singer Eric Burdon's band War. Charles Mingus arrived on stage waving a brown envelope from the tax office, furiously roaring 'I've had a letter from your Queen' - a tax demand for work on his last visit to Britain years previously. The vast Stan Kenton band's show was lit by car batteries and candles during the power cuts of the strike-bound 'winter of discontent' in 1972.

The club was now an institution, a place on the London social circuit revellers would visit whether they were jazz fans or not. Princess Margaret came, and regular visitor Spike Milligan (a former trumpeter and a close friend of Ronnie Scott's) persuaded Scott to tell a risque joke about her relationship with the actor Peter Sellers that led to indignant complaints from the national newspapers. 'We're fashionable now,' doorman Jeff Ellison said to Scott. 'With visitors like her it'll make all the difference to the place.' 'Who needs fashionable?' Scott replied. 'It means you're in for five minutes, then people forget all about you. We'll go on the way we've always done.'

'At the time, I wrote about Ornette Coleman in the Second Opinion column in Melody Maker: "I know of no other musician who has the ability to make my heart sing so." Not everybody thought that then, there was a lot of hostility to him in the conventional modern jazz community. So it was very important that Ronnie Scott's took a risk and put him on.'

VAL WILMER

**ORNETTE COLEMAN** with
**CHARLES MOFFETT** on drums 1966
Ph. VAL WILMER

**HORACE SILVER** 1966
Ph. VAL WILMER

**LEE KONITZ** 1966
Ph. VAL WILMER

'He probably came out of the womb looking cool. He and Pete always gave complete carte blanche to photographers who they felt appreciated the music. And I, as many, have been blessed to hear some of the best music ever created on the planet at their club.'

VAL WILMER

**RONNIE SCOTT** 1966
Ph. VAL WILMER

**MAX ROACH GROUP**
**MAX ROACH**
**JYMMIE MERRITT**
**ODEAN POPE**
**CHARLES TOLLIVER**
**STANLEY COWELL** (on piano) 1967
Ph. VAL WILMER

**ROLAND KIRK** 1967
Ph. VAL WILMER

'I can hear that sound now, it was like listening to God speaking. Everybody listened to every sound he made, even when he was older and more frail. You knew it was an unqualified privelege, to be there to hear the tenor sax master speak.'

VAL WILMER

**COLEMAN HAWKINS** 1967
Ph. VAL WILMER

'Vi Redd's father was a New Orleans drummer who'd been to England with Kid Ory's band. She had it all. She could come out and sing the blues, but she could play the alto saxophone like Bird.'

VAL WILMER

**VI REDD** 1967
Ph. VAL WILMER

**JOE HENDERSON** and **DAVE HOLLAND** 1968
Ph. VAL WILMER

'Illinois Jaquet was shouting from the stage "hey Red, come on up and take our picture" when this image was taken. He'd been drinking whisky at my studio earlier in the day, and had come down to join Ben Webster, who was just starting his season. Things could be pretty relaxed in those days.'

DAVID REDFERN

**BEN WEBSTER** with
**ILLINOIS JAQUET** 1969
Ph. DAVID REDFERN

**BEN WEBSTER** 1969
Ph. DAVID REDFERN

'A thrilling player, a great bandleader - and a great professional, who understood other professionals. You wouldn't get any of that fussiness about photographers from him. "Come and sit in the trombone section if you want to get a picture," he'd say to me. Of course, I never did.'

DAVID REDFERN

**BUDDY RICH** 1969
Ph. DAVID REDFERN

**CATHY** 1967
Ph. DAVID REDFERN
Buddy Rich's daughter singing at the club

'Miles didn't play a season at Ronnie's, but recorded for TV there in the late '60s. We were totally in awe watching him. He wouldn't do a sound-check but walked in ten minutes before the recording started, and just went straight for it. The set was fantastic, of course.'

DAVID REDFERN

**MILES DAVIS** 1969
Ph. DAVID REDFERN

SARAH VAUGHAN 1969
Ph. DAVID REDFERN

**RONNIE SCOTT** and
**TONY CROMBIE** 1970s
Ph. DAVID REDFERN

**BILL EVANS** 1972
Ph. VAL WILMER

**OSCAR PETERSON** 1974
Ph. DAVID REDFERN

**RONNIE SCOTT** 1970s
Ph. DAVID REDFERN

**IRENE REID** 1970s
Ph. DAVID REDFERN

'When Dizzy Gillespie was there with his big band, it was one of the most amazing things I'd ever heard at the club. That wall of noise, it went right through you.'

DAVID REDFERN

**DIZZY GILLESPIE** 1974
Ph. DAVID REDFERN

**DIZZY GILLESPIE** 1976
Ph. VAL WILMER
Playing chess with Ronnie Scott

'The expression on Billy's face says it all. He always gave a hundred percent of his effort, he loved music and he loved people
He was like Coltrane, a person who showed you how you could change your life - a musician to raise yourself by.'

VAL WILMER

**BILLY HIGGINS** 1976
Ph. VAL WILMER

**STAN GETZ** 1977
Ph. DAVID REDFERN

**CHICO FREEMAN** 1977
Ph. VAL WILMER

**RONNIE SCOTT** 1979
Ph. DAVID REDFERN

**JOHNNY GRIFFIN** 1979
Ph. DAVID REDFERN

**TONY CROMBIE**
**RONNIE SCOTT**
**MIKE CARR** 1979
Ph. DAVID REDFERN

"Eat, drink and enjoy yourselves, pretend you're on the Titanic."

RONNIE SCOTT

BUDDY RICH 1980
Ph. DAVID REDFERN

By 1980, the future of the Ronnie Scott's Club had come to look distinctly shaky. 'Eat, drink and enjoy yourselves,' Scott would tell audiences. 'Pretend you're on the Titanic.' The government introduced Value Added Tax (VAT) and Scott and King, their minds set only on presenting jazz to jazz-lovers, ignored it - until one day they got a bill for £40,000. 'If you'd been shrewd businessmen, you'd have seen this coming,' somebody said to King. 'If we'd been shrewd businessmen, we wouldn't be here at all,' King had responded.

The receivers came in in July 1980, and it looked like the end for the club. But the proprietors didn't flinch. Scott was asked by the officials if he wanted to continue or quit. He threw the question back to Pete King, always his oracle on matters of business. 'I want to go on,' King said. 'I don't know what else to do.' 'Then we continue,' Ronnie Scott concluded.

The word got around. People who felt they owed Ronnie Scott's Club a debt of gratitude for all the wonderful music it had brought them over the years chipped in any way they could. Chris Blackwell, boss of Island Records, took Pete King aside one night and simply told him he was in for £25,000 with no strings attached except that the proprietors continue to run the place the same way they always had. King recalled that he felt a rare thing for him, a tear in the eye, as Blackwell walked away. The Musicians Union, with help from jazz-loving officials Brian Blain and Johnny Patrick, helped out too. So did the brewery Charrington's, and the Performing Rights Society. The proprietors developed a membership scheme to make it cheaper to visit during the weekdays. And when a revival of popular interest in jazz, sparked by a charismatic younger generation of players, began in the 1980s, Ronnie Scott's Club was still there to present the best of it.

One of the most regular guests over the years was drummer and gifted talent-scout Art Blakey with his hot and gospelly Jazz Messengers band. Blakey became one of the icons of the latest jazz renaissance - not least because it was Blakey who introduced a teenage Wynton Marsalis to Britain at Ronnie Scott's. Audiences also poured on to the premises for a series of seasons by the spinetinglingly dramatic and hauntingly soulful singer-pianist Nina Simone. Sometimes Simone would show up straight from a cab, maybe in a fur coat and trainers, park a plastic shopping bag by the piano and just play. Her music seemed to go to the roots of the thrill that Ronnie Scott and Pete King had first felt in African-American music and jazz 40 years before, and she mingled it unpredictably with classical music, swing, and the European cabaret songs of Kurt Weill and Edith Piaf.

A fragile and prematurely aged Chet Baker, one of the romantic heroes of the

1950s 'cool school' jazz movement, delivered some moving performances at the club in the last years of his life. Baker would sometimes huddle up among the drumkits in the back office like a child, even be terrified to go out - yet often play, as Scott put it, 'like an angel.' But everyone allowed to occupy that back room behind the stage at Frith Street knew how difficult the jazz life could be, with its obligation on a travelling performer to make a spontaneous and often unrehearsed music catch light in front of a strange audience, in a strange town, over and over again for years.

The club celebrated its 25th anniversary in October 1984, and the following year saw the development of one of the strangest of all the strange twists in the history of Ronnie Scott's. On the one hand, two individualistic and unsentimental small-businessmen struggling in grimy night-time London to run an unsubsidised jazz club. On the other, a group of beleagured socialists on a sun-struck Caribbean island selling an exotic, extravagant, dance-oriented and state-subsidised music. Pete King and his wife Stella were invited to Cuba for a holiday in 1985, following an earlier visit there by Ronnie Scott as a performer. Isolated by the American trade embargo, the Cubans now wanted to promote cultural relations with western countries. Ronnie Scott had been knocked out by the quality of the Cubans' music, and at the Havana Jazz Festival on his own visit, King saw exactly what he had meant. Though both men had encountered Cuban music in London long before, in the work of club guests Machito and Mongo Santamaria, this was fiery, contemporary and different - particularly pianist Chucho Valdes and his dynamic band Irakere.

King struck a deal to bring a selection of Cuban musicians to the club. The quality was high, but the prices were not - a welcome relief, since Ronnie Scott's was increasingly running into the downside of the 'jazz boom', with many big artists becoming too expensive to hire at club rates, preferring to play concert halls for bigger fees, and at more sociable hours.

And so the musical menu at Frith Street began to change. The old favourites of many years continued to anchor the annual programme of course - like Brazilian percussionist Airto Moreira and his singer wife Flora Purim, Art Blakey's Jazz Messengers, the inventive and frequently hilarious former Dizzy Gillespie saxophonist James Moody - and the legendary Gillespie himself, still a tirelessly inventive performer though well into his sixties by now, and a regular chess partner of Ronnie Scott's in that back-room office too. But in between came fresh new bands, countering the belief in some quarters that Ronnie Scott's was getting set in its ways. Cuban mini-festivals began in Frith Street, featuring the cream of the island's new jazz talent. And, with the British Musicians' Union's financial help, the spirited and unconventional young London big band Loose Tubes arrived, bringing with it a younger audience that didn't necessarily know, or care, whether what it was hearing counted as jazz or not.

Loose Tubes played African music, bebop, soca, funk, rock, free-jazz, circus music. Rolling Stones drummer Charlie Watts' big band, on the other hand, stayed closer to a conventional jazz repertoire - but not with a conventional approach, since Watts brought together an eclectic collection of British swingers, boppers and free-jazz mavericks to play it. Stan Tracey was in the band, local tenor giant Don Weller, and a teenager and budding tenor giant hardly anyone had heard of yet - Courtney Pine. Watts stumped up £30,000 to put his dream band on, leading him to quip from the stage 'I had to buy the club for this.' Watts, a lifetime jazz enthusiast but a man with a modest view of his own jazz-drumming skills, enlisted some expert percussion support - he had the bop drummer Bill Eyden on one side of him, the free-jazz virtuoso John Stevens on the other. With all three steaming together, and the band in full cry, the power of the ensemble practically blew the cheering audiences into the street. On the opening night of Watts' run, the writer Richard Williams encountered Pete King at the bar. 'What do you think of it?' Williams asked the proprietor. King considered for a moment, puffed out his formidable chest, and finally said: 'Needs another couple of drummers.'

In the autumn of 1985 Jim Godbolt - a former agent and promoter and by now editor of the club's house magazine Jazz At Ronnie Scott's - organised a reunion for the musicians from the Club Eleven, for the 25th anniversary of its last gig. Just as in the old days, when the then twenty-something jazz obsessives dreamed of a 52nd Street club in the heart of London, Ronnie Scott and John Dankworth were among the stars, and Tony Crombie's engagingly languid style and Laurie Morgan's busier momentum powered the rhythm sections. Ronnie Scott was usually impatient with trips down memory lane - 'nostalgia isn't what it used to be' was his usual observation - but he played with all his old aplomb, and unmistakeably let his feelings of pleasure at the occasion show.

The club benefitted from the general improvement in the jazz climate through the late 1980s. It almost seemed like the old anxious nights of insecurity, of hanging on by a thread from week to week, were becoming a fading memory.

But then they came back to remind one of the partners that so many hard years can leave their calling card. In late April 1988, at the age of 59, Pete King had a major heart attack. There were no contingency plans for such an event. Scott had never considered running the club without his partner, and knew that getting on top of the business side was beyond him. King had made no arrangements for a substitute management. But in the event (and as Scott and King, experts in the art of improvisation, should perhaps have expected), the loyal members of staff - Bonnie, Dorothy, Monty, Jimmy and many others - made it up as they went along, and the public never noticed the difference. 'What was interesting was finding out they were there all the time,' Pete King said later. 'If you're a workaholic like me, you never think anybody else can do it like you, until you have to face it. Then you find out they can't do it like you, but that's because they do it their own way, a way you'd never have thought of.'

So the club, in its spontaneous, downbeat-optimistic, jazzlike way, ran on. Ronnie Scott kept doing the jokes, introducing the bands ('and now it's a pleasure to introduce...er...to introduce...must stop smoking that stuff, you can't remember anything'), blowing the saxophone, just like always.

'There were a few ups and downs with Wynton, who's very focused. "Who does he think he is, a star?" some people were saying at the club. "Yep," I said, "that's exactly what he is." Of course he proved that all the initial hype about him was right. He's done an enormous amount for jazz.'

DAVID REDFERN

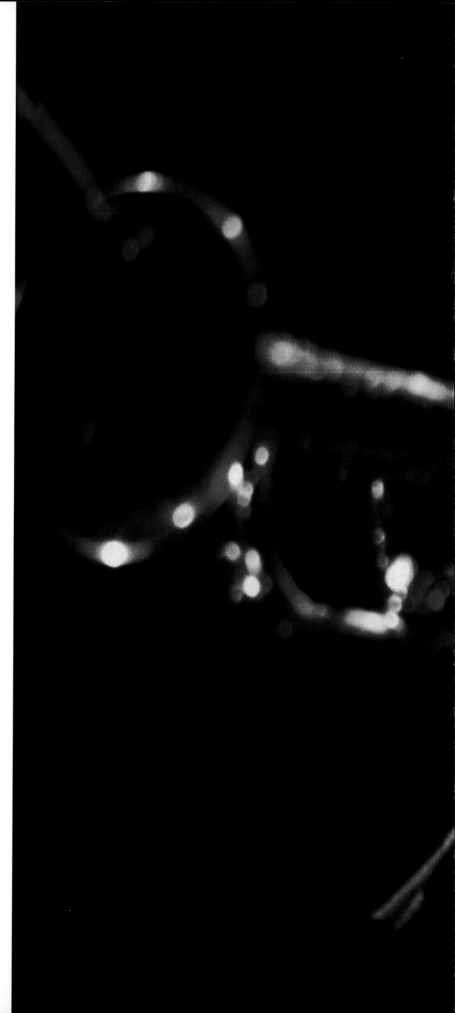

**WYNTON MARSALIS** 1983
Ph. DAVID REDFERN

**ART BLAKEY** 1983
Ph. DAVID REDFERN

**GIL EVANS** 1984
Ph. ALLAN TITMUSS

**BILLY ECKSTINE** 1984
Ph. ALLAN TITMUSS

**PETE KING, BUDDY RICH**
and **RONNIE SCOTT** 1984
Ph. DAVID REDFERN

'I had a few run-ins with Nina Simone, as a few people did. But she was amazing in performance, completely hypnotised everybody. Her appearances at Ronnie's in the '80s did a lot to turn the club around when it was in trouble. Suddenly everybody wanted to go to Ronnie Scott's and hear a legend in her prime.'

DAVID REDFERN

**NINA SIMONE** 1984
Ph. DAVID REDFERN

**NINA SIMONE** 1984
Ph. VAL WILMER

**NINA SIMONE** 1985

Ph. ALLAN TITMUSS

**RONNIE SCOTT** 1985

Ph. DAVID REDFERN

CHUCHO VALDES and IRAKERE 1985
Ph. DAVID REDFERN

BETTY CARTER 1986
Ph. ALLAN TITMUSS

**JOE PASS** 1985
Ph. ALLAN TITMUSS

**CHICK COREA** 1986
Ph. ALLAN TITMUSS

**CHET BAKER** 1986
Ph. ALLAN TITMUSS

PATRONS ARE REQUESTED TO KEEP AS
QUIET AS POSSIBLE
DURING THE ARTISTES PERFORMANCE
(Our downstairs bar is available with no such restrictions.)

**DJANGO BATES** 1986
Ph. ALLAN TITMUSS

**ARTURO SANDOVAL** 1987
Ph. DAVID REDFERN

THE LEADERS:
ARTHUR BLYTHE
CECIL McBEE
DON MOYE
LESTER BOWIE
KIRK LIGHTSEY
CHICO FREEMAN 1987
Ph. ALLAN TITMUSS

CHUCHO VALDES
ARTURO SANDOVAL
PETE KING
RON MATHEWSON
MARTIN DREW 1988
Ph. DAVID REDFERN

**AIRTO MOREIRA** 1980s
Ph. DAVID REDFERN

**CURTIS MAYFIELD** 1988
Ph. DAVID REDFERN

'Ronnie's has an amazing atmosphere. It can take anything you throw at it, big bands, anything. And it's special because it was run by musicians who put music first. Why did Ronnie and Pete start it? Certainly not to make money. And I don't know of another big jazz club in the world where you have a star attraction, and a showcase for a good local band on the same bill. '

DAVID REDFERN

**GUY BARKER** 1980s
Ph. DAVID REDFERN

**GUY BARKER** and **ALAN SKIDMORE** 1980s
Ph. DAVID REDFERN

**PETE KING** and **RONNIE SCOTT** 1989
Ph. ALLAN TITMUSS

**RONNIE SCOTT** 1988
Ph. DAVID REDFERN

# "It's a jazz club, not a shop"

RONNIE SCOTT

The club celebrated its 30th birthday in 1989 (Scott, with weary affection, called it 'a prison sentence - 30 years in a jazz club') and BBC-TV made an hour-long Omnibus documentary to herald the extraordinary achievement, with Sonny Rollins, Dizzy Gillespie, John Dankworth, Georgie Fame and many other stars lining up to express their gratitude for it. Even the British politicians John Prescott and Kenneth Clarke, jazz fans both, forgot their party differences and huddled together around a table to praise the club's contribution.

Pete King recovered and came back to his desk-job, though now on shorter hours. The 'jazz boom' accelerated. New jazz magazines sprang up, young DJs like Paul Murphy and Gilles Peterson started playing old bop albums to dancing clubbers, a radio station (JazzFM) was launched. Loose Tubes, too big and too volatile to settle into comfortable middle age, memorably played its swansong at the club in September 1990, marching out into Frith Street still playing, rounding the block of Old Compton Street and Dean Street, pulling fascinated diners out of restaurants in its wake.

But for all the jazz boom and its promise of riches, Ronnie Scott's never got suckered into changing its style. Scott and King had seen a few fashionable periods for jazz before, and didn't believe this one would last any longer than the others. The dust stayed on the lampshades, the gaffer tape still held the carpet together. Sparky young jazz entrepreneurs tried to persuade the proprietors to change their interior design, or go in for more aggressive product-marketing in the foyer. 'It's a jazz club, not a shop,' Ronnie Scott would contemptuously object. When a franchise was offered to two midlands businessmen, Alan Sartori and Barry Sherwin, to open a Ronnie Scott's on Birmingham's Broad Street, Scott initially disliked the decor and the upmarket ambiance, and for a while protested that his club's name should be dissociated from the venture. The club did open, with a Charlie Watts band its opening attraction, in autumn 1991, but the city's regular jazz audience could not sustain a dedicated jazz nightclub. After shifting to a more blues and soul-oriented programme, the venture was wound up later in the decade.

Some of the best in local and international jazz could still be heard at Frith Street however. The veteran James Moody still kept coming back to intersperse his hilariously surreal songs with his uniquely personal sax sound. Singer Betty Carter kept delivering the kind of deliriously on-the-edge jazz singing that was the very opposite of the smooth-jazz vocals styles beginning to come into fashion. Legendary composer George Russell's formidable Living Time Orchestra showed that jazz, rock and classical music could be combined without resorting to funk cliches or hot licks. At the other end of the volume slider, the quietly brilliant alto saxophonist Lee Konitz (who had played on the famous Miles Davis Birth of the Cool sessions back in 1948) and the similarly reflective British trumpet genius Kenny Wheeler could still explore an almost private musical conversation, in the expectation that the ethos of Ronnie's would accord them the respectful attention they deserved.

But after December 1996, the man who had given the club its name was no longer around to hear the great music still being made there. Ronnie Scott died suddenly at his flat in Fulham, two days before Christmas - after a dispiriting year of ill-health, dental difficulties that had hampered his saxophone-playing, and bouts of the depression that had plagued him for much of the second half of his life. Blues singer and entertainer George Melly, in the course of what the club staff always dubbed his regular 'Christmas pantomime' season, had the unenviable task of telling a shocked audience that night, absorbing the news amid the glitter of the Christmas decorations.

The event made the front pages of papers that would never consider a jazz story to be big news. The obituaries described the Scott the customers knew - the laconic, wisecracking, chainsmoking loner in a leather jacket, announcing the arrival of the world's most celebrated jazz performers in an exasperated East London drawl, as if their presence on his premises were somehow interrupting something more important, like watching the racing on TV in the back room.

But some of the tributes identified the deeper Scott, the complex, romantic, erudite and sometimes obsessive jazz-lover, with a consuming passion for the music's deceptively casual virtuosity.

The special atmosphere of Ronnie Scott's, with its mix of upmarket supper-club intimacy and tatty low-life bohemianism, had not been arrived at by calculation or market research. The ambition of Scott and King had simply been to run the kind of jazz club they'd be happy to go to themselves. The former had once called jazz 'a music of fleeting emotions', but their very elusiveness was the quality he loved. By a mixture of shrewdness, happenstance, gamblers' luck and musical insight, he and Pete King founded and ran the perfect place to let this delicate flower bloom at its colourful best. Jazz lovers and jazz musicians, of several generations, and scattered all over the globe, owe them an incalculable debt of gratitude for that.

**ROY HARGROVE** 1991

Ph. DAVID REDFERN

**LESTER BOWIE** 1993

Ph. DAVID SINCLAIR

**RONNIE SCOTT** 1993
Ph. DAVID REDFERN

HUGH MASEKELA 1994
Ph. DAVID SINCLAIR

**MACEO PARKER** 1994

Ph. DAVID REDFERN

**MARI WILSON** 1994

Ph. DAVID SINCLAIR

**CHICO FREEMAN** 1994
Ph. DAVID SINCLAIR

**DR JOHN** 1996
Ph. DAVID SINCLAIR

**ERNEST RANGLIN** 1996
Ph. DAVID SINCLAIR

**CEDAR WALTON** 1997
Ph. DAVID SINCLAIR

**ANDY SHEPPARD** 1998
Ph. DAVID SINCLAIR

**PAOLO CONTE** 1998
Ph. DAVID SINCLAIR

**JOHN HICKS** 1998
Ph. DAVID SINCLAIR

**SARAH JANE MORRIS** 1997
Ph. DAVID SINCLAIR

**DANILO PEREZ** 1998
Ph. DAVID SINCLAIR

**RANDY BRECKER** 1998
Ph. DAVID SINCLAIR

**DIANA KRALL** 1998
Ph. ALLAN TITMUSS

**BENNY GOLSON** 1998
Ph. DAVID SINCLAIR

**LIANE CARROLL** 1998
Ph. DAVID SINCLAIR

The club continues to embrace old friends and players, just as bright young newcomers embrace the club.

MARK KNOPFLER 1999
Ph. DAVID SINCLAIR

'Ronnie Scott's is not simply a jazz club,' Michael Parkinson was quoted as saying in the September 2004 edition of the inestimable house magazine *Jazz At Ronnie Scott's*. 'Rather, it is a landmark in the history of British jazz. Indeed, Ronnie Scott's is maybe *the* history of British jazz...it has survived and prospered because it has never compromised the high standards set by Ronnie and Pete right from the beginning.'

'There's no reason why it shouldn't last a hundred years and longer,' Parkinson continued. 'After all, the virtue of landmarks is that they're built to last forever.'

When Ronnie Scott died at Christmas 1996, however, many feared that sad event was to mark the end of the story. Would Pete King, after most of an adult lifetime devoted to the club, a warning heart attack, and a lengthening list of bills and legal obligations attendant on running a West End night-spot, want to continue with his friend and partner gone? Would the public conclude from the news stories that the captain and the ship would inevitably have gone down together, and simply stop showing up at Frith Street? Could the will to do the impossible and run an establishment devoted to unpredictable and uncommercial music possibly be there any more?

Nobody should have worried. The sign above the door of 47 Frith Street still stayed brightly lit. Pete King continued his imperturbable way, doing what he believed Ronnie Scott would have wanted - presenting the best jazz the club could afford, in the best conditions. In the first days of the post-Scott era at Ronnie's - and with typical breadth of view - the club followed George Melly's and John Chilton's rollicking traditional programme with the atmospheric and totally contrasting world-jazz of Brazilian percussionist Airto Moreira in January 1997. Moreira's mimicry of bird-sounds, rainstorms, or animals in an imaginary undergrowth captivated the audiences as surely as Melly's earthy blues music had done. Moreira and his singer wife Flora Purim, long-time friends of the club, had been among the first to send their condolencies and good wishes to Pete King, and express their fervent hope that the club should continue as a tribute to Scott's memory.

And continue it did, with some of its most prestigious and exciting guests arriving as the 20th century that embraced the lifetime of jazz drew to a close. Keyboard star Joe Zawinul returned to Frith Street in 1998 for the first time since his legendary fusion band Weather Report had made its British debut there twenty-six years earlier. In the same year, singer-pianist Diana Krall performed to packed houses at the club, though her international superstar status was yet to come. It was one of the last chances London had to hear Krall at close range in a supper-club setting, remoulding classic lyrics with her unique mixture of fragile lyricism and faint apprehensiveness, as if their old meanings were being experienced afresh by this subtly powerful artist.

In 1999, another landmark came and went. The 40th anniversary year was blighted by more sad losses - this time one of the club's favourite singers, Betty Carter, and one of its oldest friends, Benny Green - but two high-profile celebratory concerts at the Barbican hall featured some of the biggest names on the international circuit, including Sonny Rollins, Elvin Jones and George Benson. In a deft touch, the Frith Street club's front desk was recreated at the side of the Barbican stage, with the regular door-staff pretending to answer the phones, and Fast Show comic John Thomson making the announcements in the Fast Show's languid and exaggeratedly hip 'Jazz Club' manner.

Jazz didn't exactly enter the cultural mainstream after the turn of the millenium - most people you might stop in the street would still be unlikely to have heard of most of its stars, once you'd got past Louis Armstrong, Miles Davis, Ella Fitzgerald and maybe a handful of others. But the year 2000 saw Louis Armstrong's widely publicised centenary, American film-maker Ken Burns' big-budget, multi-part TV documentary 'Jazz', more airtime for jazz from BBC Radios 2 and 3, and the arrival of the BBC Jazz Awards ceremony as a high-profile acknowledgement of home grown talent embracing most of the music's diverse styles. With its double-bill policy of booking British artists on the same programmes as international guests, Ronnie Scott's had done much to seed the talent the BBC Jazz Awards event was now embracing.

Pete King came to Frith Street three days a week now, happy to rely on the club's full-time staff to run the show, but continuing to contribute his wealth of experience, and his constructively caustic wit, to discussions about policy and programming. A wider group of expert well-wishers and advisers began to be drawn into what had previously been more or less private deliberations between King and Ronnie Scott, bringing with them news of new developments in the music. The veteran editor and historian Jim Godbolt continued to run 'Jazz At Ronnie Scott's', the house magazine, with a variety of editorial assistants as his sight failed him. His intuitions about what entertained and informed jazz fans, however, were as sharp as ever.

At the end of 2003, the young Canadian jazz vocalist Michael Bublé - who had, with shrewd affection, fashioned hit remakes of classics like 'Fever', 'The Way You Look Tonight' and Van Morrison's 'Moondance' that year - played one of the biggest-selling club seasons ever, with crowds queueing down Frith Street to hear him. Bublé

- and Jamie Cullum and Katie Melua in Britain - were bright young newcomers into the jazz fold, with their obvious enthusiasm for jazz history and their infectious capacity to swing. Not everybody agreed that what they were doing was jazz, of course. But at Ronnie Scott's, you could still get plenty of confirmation that jazz as its more pure-minded devotees understood it, was still alive and well - even if time was sadly shortening the list of indisputable jazz pioneers still able to take the Frith Street stage. The strong and muscular music of drum giant Elvin Jones, recalling the great hard-bop bands and their evolution into the passionate music of John Coltrane, was stilled in 2004, and to Pete King and 'the family' at Ronnie's, the news of Jones' death felt like a personal loss, the breaking of another link with a magical past. And yet the beat goes on.

The Cuban connection was sustained in 2004 by a long visit from pianist Chucho Valdes, the first Cuban import with Irakere almost 20 years earlier. And the evolution of jazz into a world-music of extraordinary range and depth, seamlessly blending improvised sounds from Africa, South America, north America, Cuba, Europe and India could hardly have been more powerfully expressed than in Joe Zawinul's Syndicate. That ensemble's week-long residency in May 2004 was a standing-room-only event at Frith Street, as memorable an occasion as any at the club over all those 45 years.

**HEATH BROTHERS** 1999
Ph. DAVID SINCLAIR

**STACEY KENT** 2000
Ph. DAVID SINCLAIR

**REGINA CARTER** 1999
Ph. DAVID SINCLAIR

**RICHARD BONA** 2000
Ph. DAVID SINCLAIR

**PEE WEE ELLIS** 2000
Ph. DAVID SINCLAIR

**MANU DIBANGO** 2001
Ph. DAVID SINCLAIR

'I've heard some of Branford's best playing at Ronnie's. When the audience is five yards away, rather than fifteen in a concert hall, something special is happening, and it feeds back to the whole group.'

DAVID SINCLAIR

**BRANFORD MARSALIS** 2001
Ph. DAVID SINCLAIR

**DAVE WECKL** 2002
Ph. DAVID SINCLAIR

**LENNY WHITE** 2002
Ph. DAVID SINCLAIR

When Elvin Jones died in 2004, the news felt - to Pete King and 'the family' at Ronnie's - like a personal loss. Elvin was like a force of nature, his playing a storm of percussive energy - yet he was the gentlest of men. The news seemed to announce another broken link with a magical jazz past, but it added another 'happy ghost' to the spirit of Ronnie's.

ANDY BEY 2002
Ph. DAVID SINCLAIR

**LISA STANSFIELD** 2002
Ph. DAVID SINCLAIR

**FLORA PURIM** 2002
Ph. DAVID SINCLAIR

'An enormous sound, a great player, an absolutely charming man, and a great loss. Hugely talented. Offstage, you'd find him at a drumkit, on the piano, even the double-bass as well as the saxophone. I think I have pictures of an entire Bob Berg Quartet, all him.'

DAVID SINCLAIR

**BOB BERG** 2002
Ph. DAVID SINCLAIR

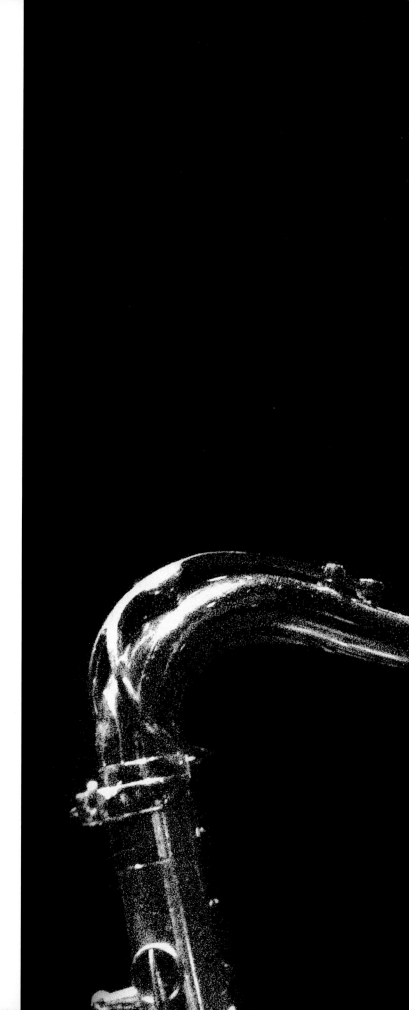

**IKE TURNER** 2002
Ph. DAVID SINCLAIR

**BILL BRUFORD** 2003
Ph. DAVID SINCLAIR

**NIGEL KENNEDY** 2003
Ph. DAVID SINCLAIR

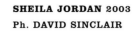

**SHEILA JORDAN** 2003
Ph. DAVID SINCLAIR

'Great players, playing Mingus's music which is some of the greatest jazz ever written. And the power of a big band in a room like Ronnie's is something you have to hear at first hand to believe.'

DAVID SINCLAIR

**SUE MINGUS** 2003
Ph. DAVID SINCLAIR

**MINGUS BIG BAND** 2003
Ph. DAVID SINCLAIR

**KENNY GARRETT** 2003
Ph. DAVID SINCLAIR

**SOWETO KINCH** 2003
Ph. DAVID SINCLAIR

**RAY GELATO** 2003
Ph. DAVID SINCLAIR

**RAVI COLTRANE** 2003
Ph. DAVID SINCLAIR

'Roy Ayers has that wonderful twinkle in the eye, it never leaves him. He loves being there, and the audience knows it.'

DAVID SINCLAIR

**ROY AYERS** 2003
Ph. DAVID SINCLAIR

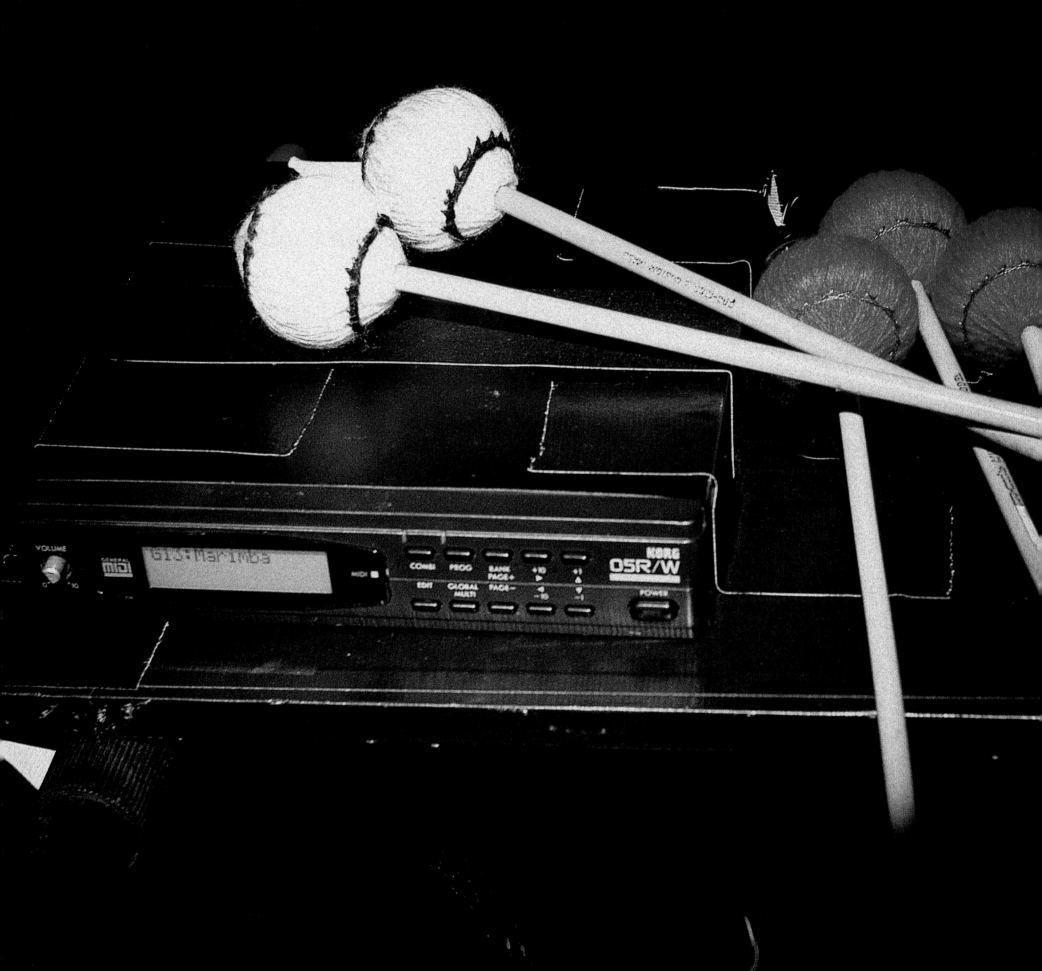

'It's sheer passion with Monty Alexander. When he isn't playing, he turns to his bassist and drummer, willing them on. It's not that he doesn't know the audience is there. But he's into the music and his group so completely, it's fascinating to watch.'

DAVID SINCLAIR

MONTY ALEXANDER 2003
Ph. DAVID SINCLAIR

'Not everybody in a Ronnie's audience is a dedicated jazz fan. Joe knows it, so he gives them a little bit of showmanship on top of all his musical skills, you really get your money's worth with him.'

DAVID SINCLAIR

JOE LOCKE 2003
Ph. DAVID SINCLAIR

**GEORGE MELLY** 2003
Ph. DAVID SINCLAIR
Melly felt Ronnie's was a place of 'happy ghosts'.

**GEORGIE FAME** 2003
Ph. DAVID SINCLAIR

**LOUIS HAYES** 2003
Ph. DAVID SINCLAIR

**HANK CRAWFORD** 2004
Ph. DAVID SINCLAIR

**DR LONNIE SMITH** 2004
Ph. DAVID SINCLAIR

**PAT MARTINO** 2004
Ph. DAVID SINCLAIR

**CHUCHO VALDES** 2004
Ph. DAVID SINCLAIR

**CHARLIE WATTS** 2004
Ph. DAVID SINCLAIR

'Carmen is totally her own person. Maybe she could be a bigger star if she sang more familiar songs. But you know as soon as she comes on, she'll be Carmen Lundy, nobody else.'

DAVID SINCLAIR

**CARMEN LUNDY** 2004
Ph. DAVID SINCLAIR

**MAYNARD FERGUSON** leading
the **FERGUSON BAND** 2004
Ph. DAVID SINCLAIR

**JEREMY PELT** 2004
Ph. DAVID SINCLAIR

**GWYNETH HERBERT** 2004
Ph. DAVID SINCLAIR

**JAMIE CULLUM** 2005
Ph. DAVID SINCLAIR

Progress toward the next milestone, the club's 45th anniversary in October, was proceeding uneventfully. Even Pete King's mock-surliness was visibly melted by the hard-swinging sound of Georgie Fame's exuberant big band, which helped the club celebrate in October. But as the 45th anniversary parties begun, Pete King announced to the press that he was bringing a powerful new voice onto the club's board - and everybody read the news as a hint that he was finally moving on.

The newcomer was Sally Greene OBE, a powerful catalyst for the regeneration of arts buildings of special interest in London, a restaurant owner, music-lover, and co-producer of the hit show 'Billy Elliot'. Greene's knowledge of the arts world and familiarity with the club, combined with the business skills to run the Old Vic and Criterion theatres and a Chelsea restaurant, seemed to make her well qualified to take Ronnie Scott's Club forward into the 21st century.

Having turned the Old Vic theatre into a charitable trust in 2000 with producer Stephen Daldry, Greene had persuaded Kevin Spacey to become artistic director there and Elton John to be Chairman. Both stars knew the music world well, with Kevin Spacey, like Sally Greene, having also been a regular at Ronnie Scott's for many years.

The next step was a hard one for Pete King, who had virtually lived in the establishment he and Ronnie had founded. But he knew that Soho was changing, and the nightclub world with it. Rents were rising faster than ever, and he was in his mid-70s with a troublesome heart to take care of - but he felt an abiding loyalty to musicians, audiences and his staff, and was determined not to let the club go to a buyer who didn't know or care about its history. Sally Greene's understanding of the importance of retaining the Club's history and integrity as a home for music and musicians convinced King that she was the right choice.

He met Greene and Spacey for tea in Covent Garden, and negotiations tentatively began. Ronnie Scott's daughter Rebecca and her mother Mary Scott were consulted about the impending change of ownership, before Sally Greene signed up for a majority share and a directorship. Putting together a four-year business plan (including the kind of attention to the kitchen and the wine-list that Scott and King had been fairly indifferent to), she guaranteed a broad commitment to the present programming, the job security of the staff and King's continuing involvement for as long as he wished.

But if the new owner believed in continuity, she nonetheless felt that audience expectations were different in the 21st century, with the old hard-core of jazz aficionados joined by a more curious and experimental general arts-goer. She wanted her club to be inclusive, and not just for buffs. If unaccompanied women couldn't be encouraged to feel at home in this bastion of a traditionally male-oriented British jazz scene, or young people persuaded that jazz was still a living and vital contemporary music, Greene would have felt that she had failed.

'I like regenerating arts spaces' Greene told The Guardian at the time. 'But I'm a traditionalist, and if a theatre has a history, like the Old Vic does, I'm determined not to dishonour it - and it's the same with Ronnie Scott's. I've been to jazz clubs all over the world, and there are none like this one.'

The Ronnie Scott's Forty Five concert was staged on October 23 2004, with appearances from the Mingus Big Band, former Art Blakey pianist Cedar Walton, soul/jazz vocalists Elkie Brooks and Liane Carroll, and good-time swing specialist Ray Gelato. A compilation double CD of music from the club came out on Universal Music, featuring world-class artists who had made big impressions at Frith Street, including Diana Krall, Wayne Shorter, Michael Brecker and Guy Barker.

When 2005 dawned, it was business as usual, with fusion star Roy Ayres and Brazilian legends Airto Moreira and Flora Purim taking up their usual seasonal places. Former Level 42 drummer (and formidable jazz pianist) Gary Husband brought his powerful Miles Davis-inspired band Force Majeure, with trumpeter Randy Brecker, and the great bebop trombonist Curtis Fuller followed in March. Cuban piano giant Chucho Valdes, classical/jazz violinist Nigel Kennedy, and Clint Eastwood's bassist son Kyle also arrived in the spring, while Sally Greene's influence grew behind the scenes.

To strengthen her board, she brought in New Zealand financier Michael Watt who became a part-shareholder in the Club. Watt was an ebullient former oilman who had moved into the media with an international sports rights group, and then into theatre production. He was a supporter of a variety of political causes around the world, and for six years had been a sponsor of the Durham Miners' Gala.

But Watt's history with Ronnie Scott's and jazz music went back a lot further. Arriving out of the blue at the Gerrard Street 'Old Place' as a globetrotting teenager in 1960, he had begun his relationship with Ronnie Scott by trying to sell him a sackful of duty-free cigarettes. Scott wouldn't pay Watt's price, but offered him a week's free entry to the club instead. Watt was already a keen jazz fan who, as he put it, 'had listened to jazz on a crystal set from the age of about nine, and thought Zoot Sims ought to be the next President of the United States'. The New Zealander thus began a close relationship with the club and its proprietors that was to flourish down the decades. But even Ronnie Scott, with his legendary capacity to remain unfazed by almost anything, might have been surprised to discover that his ownership of his famous club would eventually embrace the once-impecunious cigarette-vendor from the Antipodes.

Out front, charismatic singer Carmen Lundy and violin virtuoso Regina Carter kept the audiences fascinated during the summer of 2005, and the Ronnie's year unfolded smoothly with a series of high-class artists of very different kinds, from bop guitar star Pat Martino to vivacious singer/pianist Diane Schuur. But Sally Greene's plans were moving up a gear. In search of the perfect space to soak up the unique atmosphere she associated with Ronnie Scott's, Sally Greene contacted Paris-based French/Spanish interior designer Jacques Garcia out of the blue, having been impressed by his work on a number of Paris clubs. Garcia loved the room's most famous feature, its wall-to-wall gallery of photographs of jazz legends. And in February 2006 a major makeover began. 'I left it to him' Sally said. 'My only instruction was that the original spirit and atmosphere of the place had to be preserved.'

After a £2.38 million investment, the refurbished Club re-opened on June 26 to great acclaim. Garcia had moved the bar from the left side of the main room to the back, which helped to focus audience attention on the stage. The old gaffer-taped furniture had been replaced by luxurious red plush tiers either side of the stage, the food improved, and the makeover went down well with the press. 'Jazz's history is littered with comfortable, slightly down-at-heel clubs which have been ruined by ambitious makeovers' the critic and musician Dave Gelly noted in The Observer. 'But the revamped Ronnie's opened with a flourish on Monday night, and it was a joy to see.'

**SALLY GREENE & MIKE WATT** 2006
Ph. DAVID SINCLAIR

**RONNIE SCOTT'S REFIT** 2006
Ph. DAVID SINCLAIR

**WYNTON MARSALIS REOPENING RONNIE SCOTTS JAZZ CLUB,** JUNE 2006
Ph. DAVID SINCLAIR

VAN MORRISON 2007
Ph. DAVID SINCLAIR

CY GREY 2007
DAVID REDFERN

HIROMI 2007
Ph. DAVID SINCLAIR

GEOFF BECK & ERIC CLAPTON 2007
Ph. DAVID REDFERN

Pete King's son Chris oversaw the relaunch and the first guest in the renewed premises was the much-loved Caribbean jazz pianist Monty Alexander. Alexander paid plenty of touching tributes to the history of the place in his announcements on his opening show, a vivacious mix of ballads, swing, boogie and calypso. Most movingly, he hailed the achievements of Pete King, who was a guest of honour in the opening night crowd.

The club had certainly changed, but in line with the new owner's commitment to customer satisfaction. A popular modification was to the set-times, which were now more accessible to those with early obligations the next day. A more controversial change was the substitution of a new house-band - the Ronnie Scott's All Stars - for the ever-changing rota of local support groups that had shared the stage with the stars in the past. Former Jools Holland sax-player Leo Green (son of the club's longtime friend, the late broadcaster and author Benny Green) was hired to take on the venue's programming, and he brought in James Pearson, an engaging and highly-skilled young pianist, to run the regular support act.

Pearson, however, turned out to be a real find. The sharp-eared had picked him up as a potential star performer back in the mid-1990s at London's Guildhall School of Music, but though it took him a decade to make his entertaining and accessible debut album 'The Best Things In Life', some of the UK jazz scene's brightest luminaries considered it well worth the wait. Sir John Dankworth felt that Pearson 'showed signs of true greatness in the making', and The Observer's Dave Gelly wrote: 'this is the kind of jazz piano album anyone can enjoy'. In the Ronnie Scott's context, Gelly also perspicaciously pointed out that 'other musicians, especially singers, queue up for James Pearson's services, which is probably why he has reached the age of 34 before releasing a CD under his own name.'

Along with the relaunch, the club was announcing a dazzling roster of international stars for the summer - including popular soul-saxist David Sanborn, trumpeter Wynton Marsalis, and pianist Chick Corea. But, in a generally welcoming article for The Observer, Gelly drew cautionary attention to some simple jazz-club economics. The club held 220 people seated, with standing room for 10 or 20 more. Fees, transportation and accommodation for big-time artists would be hard to cover on the revenue from such small audiences. Ticket prices were bound to rise. The Catch-22 would be the possibility they might rise so much that the average jazz fan would be priced out of the market.

At the time, however, it was a welcome return to the club's golden age, when the biggest names in jazz would routinely occupy that tiny stage. Mike Stern, Kenny Garrett, David Sanborn, jazz-funk hitmaker Ramsey Lewis and Mahavishnu Orchestra drummer Billy Cobham preceded the eagerly-awaited August visits of Wynton Marsalis and Chick Corea. Trumpeters Randy Brecker and Eddie Henderson, vocal star Van Morrison and Wynton Marsalis' gifted sax-playing brother Branford came after them.

As well as the world-class artists who graced the legendary stage in 2007, the Ronnie Scott's Jazz Awards ceremony was held in May, with broadcaster Michael Parkinson and singing star Tony Bennett among the high-profile guests. The venture brought some welcome additional publicity in the first phase of the Club's regeneration. Not that the new Ronnie Scott's wasn't sustaining a considerable momentum in its programming now, with pianists Monty Alexander and Kenny Barron, and former Miles Davis sidemen Ron Carter and Kenny Garrett among the prestigious visitors in the first half of 2007. Jimmy Scott, the extraordinary falsetto-voiced singer beloved by everyone from Billie Holiday to Lou Reed, delivered the kind of revealing set - fragile, honest, but at times immensely moving - that could only happen in such an intimate establishment as Ronnie Scott's. The dynamic young Japanese pianist Hiromi appeared, as did legendary saxist/composer Benny Golson, the fiery David Sanborn, the veteran Johnny Griffin (an old favourite of Ronnie Scott's and Pete King's), and trumpet stars Roy Hargrove and Wallace Roney.

The transcience of the general managers resulted in pianist James Pearson finding himself in an increasingly crucial anchoring role - both as a musician and increasingly as a programmer. Pearson realised that, with artists fees and budgets spiralling, the club needed attractive artists who worked for realistic prices, and through 2007 he significantly contributed to sustaining not only the club's audience, but the level of customer satisfaction driving Sally Greene.

In December 2007 however Leo Green left his role as the Clubs principlal programmer, and thereafter the club moved away from the cabaret and pop bookings that had attracted many critics and stretched the finances.

**JOHNNY GRIFFIN** 2007
Ph. DAVID REDFERN

**McCOY TYNER** 2008
Ph. DAVID REDFERN

After Leo Green's departure Sally Greene worked with James Pearson to initiate a turnaround. The members-only policy was dropped from Jacques Garcia's elegantly refurbished upstairs bar to make it more accessible to all, and it also opened its doors to musicians as London's newest after-hours jamming joint. They brought in young trombonist/singer Michael Mwenso to host new sessions, initially running on Wednesday nights with a British group taking the first set, and an open-house musical policy operating from midnight onwards. The venture quickly took off, with both established musicians and newcomers joining in. The jams were often augmented by celebrities and musicians drifting in after their shows in the main room. Reflecting a tradition established at the outset by Ronnie Scott and Pete King - with Scott a much-respected saxophonist himself, and King a former player - James Pearson was bringing the jazz focus back to the club by understanding that elusive artform and its practitioners from the inside.

The Club continued to grow. Every week brought in not only the well-known faces of revered long-term members and regulars, but new customers spanning all ages, and Pearson was booking highly-respected jazz artists. In April 2008 Simon Cooke (formerly of radio station JazzFM and a long-time fan of the music) was appointed as the new Managing Director. Cooke had done some concert promoting during his time at JazzFM, as well as years of booking live jazz into smaller venues. He had also been on the radio station's board, and knew the corporate as well as the artistic side of the business. This was a job Cooke had dreamed of for years and Sally Greene felt she had found the right person to put her vision across.

Like Sally Greene, Michael Watt and James Pearson, Cooke was focused on the ethos of the Club and that whilst high-profile earlier bookings like r&b star Craig David might bring in money, it would dissipate respect for the establishment in the jazz world. 'You can go off-piste, musically' was Cooke's opinion 'but you have to keep it in the context of what the club is. You might sell out an r&b star for a for a fortnight, but you wouldn't do it because it wouldn't be Ronnie Scott's.' Cooke said that he felt there was a 'Ronnie parrot' on his shoulder, shouting in his ear if he booked an artist who didn't live up to the club's history.

However, such a comparatively small music room couldn't survive even on 80% attendances, but needed to be regularly full. That meant ending long residencies for which audiences would tail off after a few nights, and more scientific assessment of just how many sell-out shows a particular artist could command. Cooke seemed to be a good fit at the Club and Michael Watt said of him 'he listens - he gets the best out of other people in the organisation by letting them have enough rope.' But despite his jazz enthusiasms (which run all the way from the American mainstream to Europe's nu-fusion artists like Nils Petter Molvaer and Erik Truffaz), Watt always made clear he didn't want to interfere in the newly-conceived programming. By August 2008, the upstairs bar was a popular draw for younger audiences, featuring soul, funk and jazzy dance music as well as its informal jams. The twilight world of Ronnie Scott's Club ventured out into the daylight for an outdoor Bank Holiday promotion in Richmond Park, headlined by popular singer/saxist Curtis Stigers and the Ronnie Scott's Big Band.

The 50th anniversary year of 2009 brought memorable performances from saxophonists Courtney Pine and Joshua Redman, idiosyncratic saxist/composer Don Byron, drummer Jack DeJohnette with British sax legend John Surman. There were also sell-out shows from Kyle Eastwood, Julian Joseph, Jools Holland, Nigel Kennedy, Georgie Fame, Branford Marsalis, to name a few, as well as more cutting edge British bands such as Polar Bear, Get the Blessing and Led Bib. In the upstairs room, flamenco music, Cuban dance nights, tap-dancing and poetry events brought an intrigued new audience to Frith Street. Collaborations with the British Film Institute and Getty Images Gallery on exhibitions of jazz film and photography were also new departures, as was the very successful Brit Jazz Festival in August.

Running Ronnie Scott's Club was now rather different to the early days when Ronnie or Pete could simply lift a phone and find Sonny Rollins at the other end. But beneath it all, the philosophy of the old days hadn't changed that much. 'Book great acts and make sure people know about it' was Cooke's simple philosophy, and the original proprietors would have agreed with him.

For her part, Sally Greene has no illusions about inheriting the mantle of Ronnie Scott and Pete King, the hardest double-act to follow on the international jazz scene. 'They created it, we didn't' she announces frankly. 'I'm just proud to have been able to help give such a wonderful place a new lease of life, so it can go on presenting great jazz artists in the same way it has been doing for the past 50 years. When you take over something that's iconic, it's a big learning experience to get the feel of it. We got some things right, and others we didn't at first. But in this anniversary year, I really feel it's coming together. There's a recession, but the audiences keep coming - because they want to forget their troubles, maybe, and they want to hear music of real lasting quality, in the ideal environment for it. We've got 20 year-olds coming here, we've got 90 year-olds. Wherever you go in the world, everyone's heard of this club. It's the legendary Ronnie Scott's.'

Back at the end of the 1950s, Ronnie Scott and Pete King - following little advice but their own convictions, and with blind faith taking the place of hard cash - had launched and sustained the ideal space in which to listen to the elusively fascinating music of jazz, a place in which musicians as well as fans felt at home. Ronnie Scott once described those first, almost innocent, enthusiasms for the visiting American pioneers, in a conversation we had for The Guardian newspaper. 'Those people were idols for us' Scott said. 'It was hard for us to believe we were actually talking to them, let alone hearing them play.' Scott also pointed out a crucial fact about his club, its avoidance of the carefully-rehearsed, tightly-organised cabaret performances elsewhere on the nightclub circuit. 'It gave audiences a chance to see those players' humanity' Scott said. 'That they could be wonderful, and they could also fuck up, like everybody else does. That's why it never stops being an education to me.'

**John Fordham**
Jazz critic
August 2009

**JOE LOVANO** 2008
Ph. DAVID REDFERN

**IAN SHAW** 2008
Ph. DAVID SINCLAIR

**JOSHUA REDMAN** 2009
Ph. DAVID SINCLAIR

**EDDIE HENDERSON** 2008
Ph. DAVID REDFERN

RONNIE SCOTT'S BIG BAND 2009
Ph. DAVID SINCLAIR

## THE PHOTOGRAPHERS

**John 'Hoppy' Hopkins** was a photographer during the early 1960s specialising in music, left-politics and documentary subjects. Hopkins brought the new look of 35mm available-light photography (previously, the cumbersome Rolleiflex was predominant) to the smoky clubs and cellars where folk, jazz, blues and early rock musicians hung out. Hopkins recalls he was never asked for an entry fee at Ronnie Scott's - the proprietors knew the pictures documenting Hopkins' favourite music would land up in the Melody Maker and sometimes the quality glossies. By 1966 'Hoppy' left photography to promote London's underground culture via the International Times newspaper and the legendary UFO club. In recent years his pictures have been rediscovered and re-exhibited. Nowadays he lurks with a digital Nikon. More of Hoppy's images can be found at **www.hoppy.be and gettyimages.**

**Val Wilmer** has photographed the artists who appeared at Ronnie Scott's from 1960. As a writer, her interviews and first-night reviews were also regular features of the jazz press and Melody Maker. Val Wilmer's photographs have been exhibited internationally, her work being held in many public and private collections, among them the National Portrait Gallery, London, and Musée d'Arte Moderne, Paris. Her books include The Face of Black Music, As Serious As Your Life and Portrait of the Blues.

**David Redfern** has been associated with the club for over 35 years and in this time has contributed hundreds of pictures that have become an integral part of the club's decor. At Ronnie Scott's and elsewhere, he has photographed jazz greats including Louis Armstrong, Miles Davis, Nina Simone and Duke Ellington - and in a career spanning more than 40 years (documented in his book "The Unclosed Eye - The Music Photography of David Redfern") he has witnessed and recorded the birth and rise of rock 'n' roll, the British Trad boom and all the points in between. For ten years, Frank Sinatra carried a Redfern portrait on his passport. Miles Davis once refused to be photographed until David arrived! More of David's images can be found at **www.redferns.com**

**Allan Titmuss** met Ronnie Scott backstage at the Royal Festival Hall in July 1984 during the first concert he ever photographed, and began working at the Club a few days later. One night Art Blakey lowered the club's piano lid after a Jazz Messengers' set, spread some of his pictures on top, and said "These are baaaaaaad - when you coming to New York?" Described by The Times's Picture Editor as "Taking photographs without benefit of light", Allan is the only photographer to have worked on-stage with Miles Davis, and on the Club's stage with - amongst others - Branford Marsalis, Chick Corea, Diana Krall, Chet Baker, and Betty Carter. In 1985 he took Miles's favourite picture of himself. **www.allantitmuss.com**

**David Sinclair**. Scottish. David has only been a freelance photographer since 1989, but in this time has rapidly built up a very large collection of active musical shots, mainly of jazz musicians. David's photographs of Ronnie Scott's are regularly used in The Guardian, The Times, Evening Standard and The Independent, plus various jazz magazines, particularly Jazz Hot in France, and many CD covers for labels including Blue Note. Famous for once having held Ronnie Scott's lighted cigarette for him, and for once having received a smile from Pete King. More of David's images can be found at **www.jazzphotographs.com**

## THE AUTHOR

**John Fordham** is a London-born freelance journalist. He began visiting Ronnie Scott's as a fan in 1969, and as a jazz writer for Time Out magazine from 1970. Fordham edited Time Out from 1978-81, became principal jazz critic of The Guardian in the same period (and still is), co-edited the magazine City Limits with Nigel Fountain from 1981-86 and edited the bi-monthly JazzUK from 1999-2008. He has written several books on jazz, including Ronnie Scott's biography 'Jazzman - The Amazing Story of Ronnie Scott and his Club' (Kyle Cathie 1995), and 'Jazz' (Dorling Kindersley) and has broadcast on radio and TV. He recalls that one of his first nervous greetings to Pete King was met with the enquiry "hello boy, still creeping about?". The relationship never looked back.